PRAYERS
FOR A NEW
MILLENNIUM

MARY LOU KOWNACKI, OSB

Liguori

ONE LIGUORI DRIVE
LIGUORI MO 63057-9999
314.464.2500

Author Note

Like all prayers, the ones in this booklet come from words and memories stored in the heart. As a member of a monastic community, I have been praying the psalms and other Scripture at least three times a day for nearly forty years. So, psalm phrases and Scripture verses often slipped into these millennium prayers without invitation, as familiar friends are free to do. Classic prayers from Saint Augustine ("Beauty Ever Ancient…") and Teresa of Avila ("Let Nothing Disturb Thee…") and even the Hail Mary appeared unannounced. Since I greet each day by reading a handful of poems, I was not surprised to discover a line by Gerard Manley Hopkins ("Charged with your grandeur…") or a prayer inspired by Lucille Clifton's "Let there be new flowering." But when I found Jane Kenyon's line, "Let evening come" in my prayer, I felt truly honored.

༂

ISBN 0-7648-0232-1

Cover design by Grady Gunter

Contents

Part IV: Miscellaneous Prayers

Part I

GOD THE SON

Prayer to

JESUS CHRIST: SAVIOR OF THE WORLD YESTERDAY, TODAY, AND TOMORROW

Jesus, Savior of the world,
    save my yesterday.
Help me cherish my memories.
Hold close to my heart
    the warmth of family,
    the roots of neighborhood,
    the loyalty of friendship,
    the tears of broken dreams,
    the people I wronged.
From this well of memory I draw my today.

Jesus, Savior of the world,
    save my today.
Help me
    listen to the birdsong,
    taste the noon wind,
    enjoy the scent of falling leaves,
    wonder at the closing primrose,
    touch the hand of another.
I incense the moment.
From reverence of the present
    I create my tomorrow.

Jesus, Savior of the world,
    save my tomorrow.
Help me understand the futility
    of organizing my days,
    of fearing the turn of the corner,
    of dreading the marathon of old age.

Ah yes. *Let evening come.*
I rejoice in sunset and morning star.
Into your hands I commend my tomorrow.

℘

Prayer from
SCRIPTURE

Listen: If today you hear God's voice,
    harden not your heart.
Listen: If today you hear God's voice,
    poison not your tongue.
Listen: If today you hear God's voice,
    close not your imagination.
Listen: If today you hear God's voice,
    judge not the speck in the neighbor's eye.
Listen: If today you hear God's voice,
    kneel and kiss the earth
      speak the truth
        walk in beauty
          love with extravagance.

℘

Prayer for
CHRISTIAN UNITY

We come to your banquet, Jesus,
but we sit at reserved places.
We wait for you
to reenter the temple
and overturn our separate tables,
casting out centuries of suspicion, hurt,
    and distrust,

casting out dogmas we have killed for,
casting out harsh creeds that have hardened
  our hearts.

Clothe us in new wedding garments, Jesus.
Seat us at one banquet table, Jesus.
Raise the cup once again.
Insist that we remember you together
  in the breaking of the bread.

ॐ

Prayer for
HOLINESS

"My eyes grow weary searching for God."
Like the psalmist from ages past,
  I look for you in creeds and catechisms.
  I search for you in miracles and visions.
  I watch for you in prayer and stillness.
  I gaze upon you in tabernacle and host.
  I seek you in Scripture and story.
  I glimpse you in ocean and insect.
  I behold you in pilgrim and beggar.

My eyes grow weary searching for you, O God.

ॐ

Prayer for
A DEEPER UNDERSANDING
OF THE INCARNATION

The Incarnation is no mystery, Jesus.
You make it easy to understand.
Because you walked our earth
we are to see the face of the Divine

in every person we meet:
    the friend who betrayed
    the family gathered for a meal
    the welfare mother
    the man on death row
    the clerk in the store
    the teenage thug on the corner
    those my government calls enemy
        and trains me to kill.

Every time I love,
    the mystery of the Incarnation happens.
Every time I love,
    I birth you on earth, Jesus.
I fall on my knees and beg you, Jesus,
    deepen my living of the Incarnation.

෫෭

Prayer for
RENEWAL OF BAPTISMAL VOWS

I baptize you.
I draw water.
I pour water.
Water rushes down the mountainside,
surges through the streams;
fountain upon fountain from the wellspring,
water flowing from the bedrock.
I taste water.
All the waters of earth
flood life into the dry bed of my soul—
like when your cousin, John,
plunged you into the Jordan, Jesus,
and the scroll of Isaiah unrolled

in the deep.
Like that, the Spirit comes upon me
sending me to preach
    good news to the poor,
    liberty to those in chains,
    sight to the blind,
    and to set free the oppressed.
I drink the flowing waters.
    I am water flowing.
The drylands break into fruit.
    I am water flowing.
The dry bones break into dance.
    I am water flowing.

ॐ

Prayer to
SHE WHO IS

Mother of dark soil,
    morning star,
    and vast ocean—
Mother who births plants,
    winged creatures,
    fishes,
    and four-footed beasts—
Mother who nurses the stars,
    the planets,
    the black universe—
Mother who suckles the children of earth—
Mother who holds creation in strong arms,
    rocking it through the ages
    with the lullaby of life—
Show us your face, O Divine Mother.
Show us your face.

Part II
GOD THE HOLY SPIRIT

Prayer to
THE HOLY SPIRIT:
THE PERSON-LOVE, THE UNCREATED GIFT

O Uncreated Gift,
O Pure Taste of Love,
awaken in us a reverence for life.
Pour your spirit within us
until we are filled and overflowing
with life—
    abundant life.

O Most Precious Gift,
    to cherish the sunflower—
    to pray the wind—
    to protect the defenseless—
    to honor the womb-child—
    let this be our never-ending praise:
      All is Gift. All is Gift.

ॐ

Prayer of
GRATITUDE FOR
TECHNOLOGICAL ADVANCES

Let no technological wonder
disturb you.
Let no scientific breakthrough
frighten you.
None.
Not laser beams.
Not implants.
Not cyberspace.
Not cloning.

None.
All technology is limited.

The Spirit alone is limitless.
Wonder attains enlightenment.
One who has God is filled with awe.
Behold, God alone makes all things new.

❧

Prayer for
ENVIRONMENTAL AWARENESS
AND RESPONSIBILITY

O Holy Spirit, come to us.
Come, bring the children.
Pour each a cupful of spring water.
Say to them, "This is how water tastes."

Come, bring the children.
Climb a hill together.
Breathe in pure air.
Say to them, "Air, this is air."

Come, bring the children.
Find a sun-drenched place in the forest.
Say to them, "Listen. Let the trees
     speak their story."

Come, bring the children.
Stand under a star-spangled sky.
Say to them, "Be still."

Come, bring the children.
Kneel and kiss the earth.
Say it simply: "This is your mother."

O Holy Spirit, come to us.

Prayer for
THE RESTORATION OF PEACE AND JUSTICE

Holy Spirit, it is time.
The children are hungry,
and the poor can no longer plant hope.

Your promise
to fill the poor with good things
and the rich send empty away
goes unfulfilled.
It is an embarrassment,
a laughingstock,
a mockery of sacred promise.

Now overtake our hearts with your fire.
On earth let the flame of justice
leap wildly.
Release in us
a brilliant blaze of compassion.
Let the fires burn away
    all pettiness, greed, selfishness,
        and lust for security.
Let embers of kindness fill the land.

Whoever holds a debt, it will be forgiven.
Whoever is rich will give half away:
land returned to the peasant,
prison doors thrown open,
military budgets dissolved,
a cup of water given in Jesus' name.
Again. Again. And yet again.
Amen

Prayer for
CHRISTIAN UNITY

Let there be a new spirit
in the Church
of Jesus.
Let the spirit be a song
of many voices.
Let each voice
sing a melody strong and pure.
Let the melodies
blend in rich sound
filling the churches.

Let the sound
rush through stained glass windows
pouring notes of hope
into the streets.
Let the notes of hope
   heal hearts,
   restore broken dreams,
   inspire the human spirit.

Let us be a new song unto the Spirit.
Let us be a new song.

ॐ

Prayer for
UNITY WITHIN THE CHURCH

How good it is for us, God,
to live together in unity.
It is like wine, choice red wine
flowing at a family feast,
where talk of women's ordination,

divorce,
birth control,
and the meaning of resurrection,
opens hearts,
challenges sight,
strains ideas,
stretches bonds
until
we fill the goblets and toast aloud:
    We believe.
    We break bread.
    We bind wounds.
    How good it is for us
    to live together in unity.

ॐ

At Prayer with MARY

Come, Spirit,
make me docile to your voice.
Help me debate angels.
Let your will be done in me
even if it means
    misunderstanding,
    rejection,
    scandal.
Give me wisdom to find you
in the irrational:
    heavens gone awry,
    astrologers' predictions,
    songs in the night.
Give me such hospitality of heart that
    family,

foreign seers,
poor shepherds and animals
find a home in my presence.
Let me protect innocent children from
oppressive power.
Make me fearless of foreign lands and
unknown journeys.
When I cannot find you
do not let me rest until I search
home,
highway,
and temple.
Let me always insist on miracles to
celebrate love.
And when all I love on earth
lies lifeless in my arms
let me offer it to you with such freedom
of heart
that I am swept up into the heavens.
Amen

Part *III*
GOD THE FATHER

Prayer to
GOD THE FATHER OF
OUR LORD JESUS CHRIST

Are you ever lonely
God the Father?
You—who while the clay was still moist,
recognized that it would not be good
for Adam to be alone—
have lived in the heavens
and the hearts of your faithful
alone for two millenniums.
You sit in church frescoes
like a bachelor grandfather,
benevolent but remote,
your white beard growing longer
with each passing day.
Adam needed you to create the woman
and bring him to completion.
Do you need us, God our Father,
    to form your feminine face,
    to praise your mother-side,
    to honor your maternal deeds?
Are you yearning for the day
when God our Mother
is born in you?

Prayer for
CONVERSION: FROM CHOOSING SIN TO CHOOSING GOOD

In youth it was clearer, God.
There was evil and goodness,
   mortal sin and grace,
   the evil and virtuous,
   the saved and the lost.
I knew the enemy and attacked
with all the pompous self-righteousness
of one who is certain of divine revelation.

Maybe it was trying to listen
   with the ear of my heart.
Maybe it was repeating the chant:
   "Turn my heart of stone to a heart of flesh."
Maybe it is looking in the mirror
   day after day.

All I know is that my tears
fall more freely now,
turning a black and white world
into shades of gray.
I still pray for conversion of heart.
I still pray to choose good over evil.
My deepest plea, though,
is not to hurt another
in the pursuit of any truth.
With the mystic I pray,
Do you want to be a saint?
   Be kind. Be kind. Be kind.

Prayer for
CHARITY AND A PREFERENTIAL OPTION FOR THE POOR

Poor Ones,
Please take the bread.
It is yours.
The house with running water
belongs to you.
A plot of land, a dignified job—
all yours.
Forgive me for offering it.
Charity is no substitute for justice
but your children are hungry now.

Spirit of Justice,
break open our hearts.
Break them wide open.
Let anger pour through
   like strong winds,
    cleansing us of complacency.
Let courage pour through
   like spring storms,
    flooding out fear.
Let zeal pour through
   like blazing summer sun,
    filling us with passion.
Force of Justice, grant me us
   anger at what is,
   courage to do what must be done.
   passion to break down the walls
   of injustice
    and build a land flowing

with milk and honey
for God's beloved,
God's special love,
God's Poor Ones.

Spirit of Justice,
break open our hearts.

୬

Prayer for
MEETING THE CHALLENGE
OF SECULARISM

Be watchful.
Like thieves in the night
the disciples of secularism—
    those who see no spirit in the clay—
come to rob us of the Divine.
Under the guise of enlightenment
they steal our souls.
Rid of mystery and meaning,
all life is diminished,
    reduced to mirror reflection.

O Beauty ancient, ever new,
I believe that all creation
is *charged with your grandeur.*
I beg to see your glory
    in every face,
    in every flower,
    in every fortune.

I beg to see it forever.
Amen

Prayer for
DIALOGUE WITH GREATER RELIGIONS

I bow to the one who signs the cross.
I bow to the one who sits with the Buddha.
I bow to the one who wails at the wall.
I bow to the OM flowing in the Ganges.
I bow to the one who faces Mecca,
 whose forehead touches holy ground.
I bow to dervishes whirling in mystical wind.
I bow to the north,
 to the south,
 to the east,
 to the west.
I bow to the God within each heart.
I bow to epiphany,
 to God's face revealed.
I bow. I bow. I bow.

౼

Prayer for
INTERIOR IMPROVEMENT

If today you hear God's voice,
harden not your heart.

When I heard a voice
in the strange dream,
I entered a land unknown.

When the mysterious star appeared,
I followed it through the night
to the stable of the poor.

When the stranger knocked
on my door,
he begged for bread and shelter.

When the wild angel arrived,
she placed a flaming sword of justice
in my hand.

When I entered the burning bush,
you told me
that where I stand is holy ground.

When the writing formed
in the palm of my hand,
I knew my true name.

If today you hear God's voice,
harden not your heart.

၉ာ

Prayer to MARY

Too easily the words
trip off the tongue:
Mary, model of love.
But my hands tremble,
    my knees grow weak
when I pray these words.
Mary, if you are
    the model of love,
I fear to follow you.

I want my good name
    and my reputation.

I want loved ones
     to comfort me in old age
     and stand near
     when death arrives.

Deliver me from aged prophets
     and blind women seers
     who haunt temples
     and sing my praises
     while driving a sword
     through my heart.
"Thy will be done"
is not a prayer I wish
to whisper to winged messengers.

Turn me into fire, Mary.
Melt me into pure gold.
Let me dance in the blazing flames
of God's consuming love
until I am transformed
into a person so transparent
that others see the flame of God
shining through me.
Turn me into burning love itself, Mary,
into burning love itself.

Part IV
MISCELLANEOUS
PRAYERS

Prayer for
THE CHILDREN

Let us save…
  pomegranates, kind words, a baby's cry, the
  dolphin outjumping a wave, a monk's chant,
  painting pictures in clouds, belief in tomorrow,
  the ozone, church bells in inner-city streets,
  warm sand on bare feet, rituals, cricket music,
  family ties.
Let us save them for the children.

Let us save…
  raspberry bushes, the full moon of a desert
  stretch, visions of angels, stars you can grab on
  a summer night, impossible dreams, snowflakes
  on the tongue, the family table, faithful
  friendship, fatigue after a day's work, water
  table and food chain, laughter, a passion for
  justice, the present moment.
Let us save them for the children.

Let us save…
  the white antelope, a candle flame in a dark
  chapel, the rain forest, meadows drunk with
  dandelions, a passion to end hunger, the sound
  of rain beating on plowed fields, imagination,
  kneeling to praise, wild fields of sunsets,
  reverence for life, long grasses covered with
  dew, a mother's milk, the great-hearted heron.
Let us save them for the children.
Amen

Prayer for
A CONTEMPLATIVE HEART

Be still and know that I am God.

Be in stillness
until I erupt in spontaneous awe
    at a grain of sand,
    a hollyhock in bloom,
    an ocean spray,
    the air I breathe,
    the energy of matter,
    the sacredness of being.

Be in stillness
until each person I meet
    is bathed in such light
    that I genuflect in adoration.

Be in stillness
until I dance with you, God
    in a circle of fire
    at the heart of the universe.

Be still and know that I am God.

ॐ

A Litany for
THE MILLENNIUM

O Cosmic Christ,
in you
    and through you
    and for you,
all things were created;

in you
    all things hold together
    and have their being.

Through Teilhard de Chardin,
    scientist of the cosmos,
you imagined a new heaven and a new earth.
Through Teresa of Avila,
    charismatic leader,
you inspired a church of courage and wisdom.
Through Mahatma Gandhi,
    great soul,
you became nonviolent in the struggle for justice.
Through Catherine of Siena,
    fearless visionary,
you forged a new path for women.
Through Meister Eckhart,
    creative mystic,
you refused to abandon the inner light.
Through Hildegard of Bingen,
    greenness of God,
you poured out juicy, rich grace on all creation.
Through Dr. Martin Luther King, Jr.,
    drum major of freedom,
you shattered racial barriers
    and freed dreamers to dream.
Through Anne Frank,
    writer and witness,
you preserved goodness in the midst of great evil.
Through Cesar Chavez,
    noble farmworker,
you transformed the dignity of human labor.

Through Harriet Tubman,
    prophet and pilgrim,
you led the captives into freedom.
Through Vincent Van Gogh,
    artist of light,
you revealed the sacredness
    in sunflowers
    and in starry nights.
Through Thea Bowman,
    healer songbird,
you danced the African-American culture
into the Church.
Through Pope John XXIII,
    window to the world,
you awakened awareness to the signs of the times.
Through Mother Teresa of Calcutta,
    guardian of the unwanted,
you enfleshed a reverence for all life.
Through Thomas Merton,
    universal monk,
you explored the sanctity of every human search.
Through Mary Magdalene,
    apostle to the apostles,
you ordained women to proclaim the good news.
Through Wolfgang Amadeus Mozart,
    musician of Holy Mystery,
you bathed the world in beauty.
Through Julian of Norwich,
    anchoress and seer,
you showed the Mother image of God.
Through Dom Bede Griffiths,
    marriage of East and West,
you unveiled the divine face
at the heart of the world.

Through Joan of Arc,
    defender and protector,
you remained true to personal conscience
over institutional law.
Through Rumi,
    poet in ecstasy,
you illuminated friendship as mystical union.
Through Maura Clarke and Companions,
    martyrs of El Salvador,
you rise again in the hopes of the dispossessed.
Through Rabbi Abraham Heschel,
    Hassidic sage,
you answered our search for meaning
with wonder, pathos for the poor, and sabbath
rest.
Through Dorothy Day,
    pillar of the poor,
you recognized holiness as bread for the hungry.

O Cosmic Christ,
in your heart
all history finds meaning and purpose.
In the new millennium,
    in the celebration of jubilee
help us find that which we all seek:
    a communion of love
    with each other
    and with you, the Alpha and Omega,
        the first and last,
        the yesterday, today, and tomorrow,
        the beginning without end.
        Amen